Just Call Me Fred

101 Thoughts on People, Business and Life in General

Copyright © 1998 by Meijer, Inc.

All rights reserved. Published 1998
Written permission must be secured by Meijer, Inc. to use
or reproduce any part of this book, except for brief quotations
in critical reviews or articles.

Printed in the United States of America

Illustration Credits: Back cover and illustration facing quotes 9, 17, 23, 33,
46, 52, 65, 89 — Johnson Design Group • Ada, Michigan

Photo Credits: Front cover and photograph facing quote 93 — Courtesy of
Frederik Meijer Gardens • Grand Rapids, Michigan;
Photograph facing quote 74 — Anna Moore Butzner, The Grand Rapids Press

Special thanks to H.M., J.B., L.H., K.S. and T.L.
for their coordination in the development of this book.

*You shouldn't live in fear
of stepping into something soft.
We used to follow the cows.
When it was warm,
it wasn't so bad.*

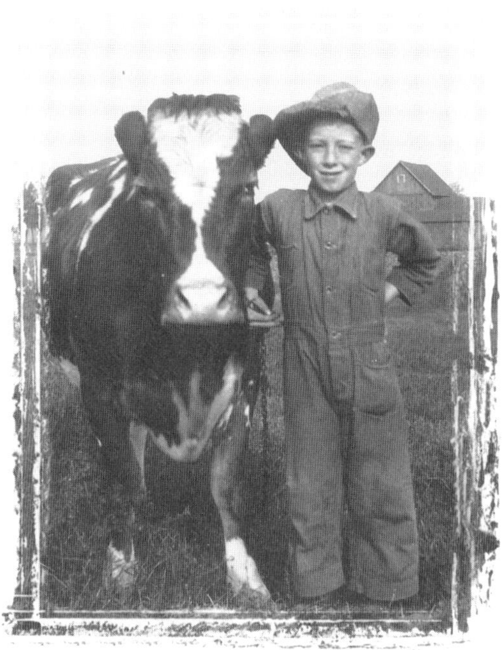

"Never say never—
never say forever"
1974 Meijer 40th
Anniversary

The future has always been
scary but challenging

3-6-69 moved into new
offices on Walker

"Growing means risking"
2-16-60 Almost merged
with Plumbs

We have to handle our challenges
and we need to have fun doing it.
Oct '63 - Cascade store destroyed by fire

Introduction

The year was 1959. America had just put her first satellite in space. I was fresh out of high school, wondering where to go to seek my fortune beyond the friendly folks of small town mid-America.

With cautious enthusiasm and the knowledge I'd learned working in our family store, I headed for the nearest city, hoping to get a job at one of the small grocery chains that were a big part of the retail scene during the late 1950s. I applied at a small, fledgling company and, surprisingly, got a job. Little did I realize that this would be my home for the rest of my working career.

I still remember my first introduction to the owner, Fred Meijer, the son of a Dutch immigrant. His friendly, easy manner felt reassuring to this scared country boy. He welcomed me into the company with only one request, *"Just call me Fred."*

Now, four decades later, I pull a worn file from my desk, full of notes scribbled on napkins (complete with coffee stains), used envelopes and scraps of paper — all written at unexpected moments, each containing practical guides to living that were spoken by Fred.

I have saved these notes over the past 40 years for two reasons. First, they have had a profound effect on who and what I believe in today. Second, they were spoken by a man who I observed always practiced what he preached. I've watched, listened and learned as these bits of wisdom came during times of crisis, pep talks and light-hearted discussions.

It was never my intention, nor do I feel adequate, to publish these notes; but by doing so now, I hope to help some other Meijer team member, supplier, customer or student of human behavior

W.S.S. note from a meeting with Fred, 1974

understand the driving principles behind the pioneer of One-Stop Shopping in the second-largest family-owned retail company in America today.

And so, out of respect for Fred, the Meijer family, Earl Holton and the institution they represent, I feel compelled to share what I have learned.

Wow! What a journey this has been — sometimes bumpy, often unpredictable, but always exhilarating. Thank you, Fred.

—*W.S.S., a student*

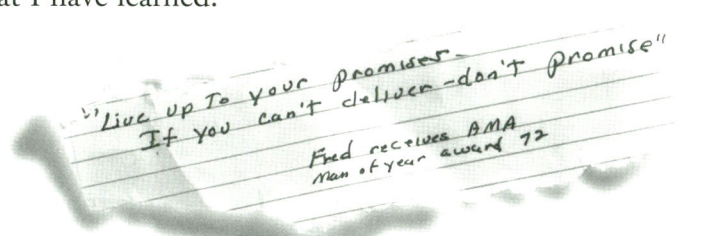

"Live up to your promises. If you can't deliver—don't promise"

Fred receives AMA Man of year award 72

W.S.S. note from a meeting with Fred, 1986

Earl and Fred

1
I've never been lonesome in my job.

2

*I was very fortunate; my father treated me with dignity.
He treated me as a person and he never bawled me out in public.*

3

If I looked okay sometimes, it usually wasn't my idea. I've always asked everyone and their uncle for advice.

4

Life is better understood backward. The problem is, you have to live it forwards.

5
Remember how you don't like to be treated.

6

*I think about the
old Chevy slogan,
"Getting there is half the fun."
I think it's all the fun.*

Just Call Me Fred

Replica of first Meijer truck

7

I never had bad breath after my father died.

8

When my dad and I wanted to accomplish something, we'd talk it over. Then he'd often send me out to do it. It was through his help that I accomplished things I otherwise might not have tried. He delegated and I learned.

*Listen to advice
and accept instruction,
and in the end you
will be wise.*

— King Solomon, Book of Proverbs

9

I get help every day from other people. They help me make better decisions and keep me from making stupid ones.

10

We used to take the customers' orders and do the running. Now the customer does the running and we take their money. I guess that's progress.

11

You must respect yourself before others can respect you.

• Just Call Me Fred •

Meijer Supermarket Grand Opening, 1952

12
Customers don't need us, we need them.

13

Some people want to research forever and never come to a decision. You must come to a decision sometime and move forward.

14

Every manager in our company has only one job — it's to help the people who report to them to be successful.

15

To be really successful, you need to have a couple of these qualities: maverick, juvenile delinquent or non-conformist.

• Just Call Me Fred •

• Just Call Me Fred •

*A good name
is more desirable than
great riches.*

— King Solomon, Book of Proverbs

16

Selling stock may be a fast way to raise capital for expansion, but I think there are more advantages to remaining a private company.

17

I was very bashful in high school. I never led anything like head of this or president of that.

• Just Call Me Fred •

Fred, with a likeness of young Fred, at Frederik Meijer Gardens

18

Intelligence without sound judgment will cause more trouble than joy.

19

People are only loyal to things they help create or improve.

• Just Call Me Fred •

20

There's nothing like being part of a winning team that's having fun.

21

If you make a mistake, make it in favor of the customer.

22

Loud orders and shouting just won't do it. It may work in the short run, but not for the long run, and we hope to be in business many, many years.

• Just Call Me Fred •

A man who loves wisdom brings joy to his father.

— King Solomon, Book of Proverbs

23

It was 1961. My dad and I were talking about whether we should start Thrifty Acres. My dad said he was too old, he thought, to see it through. Then I asked him what he would do if he were my age. He said he'd jump in with both feet — and so we did.

24

The future has always been scary but challenging.

25

Our goal isn't to see how big we can be, it isn't the number of stores; it's soundness. Our goal is to be in business 25 years from now.

Just Call Me Fred

26

*Get to know older people.
Listen to their stories.
They have wonderful experiences
— both good and bad.*

27

You should never promote someone if you're absolutely convinced that person will fail. However, once you promote someone, you should do everything you can to help that person succeed.

28

*Cultivate ideas.
If they work, give credit.
If they don't work,
take the blame yourself.*

29

Try to preserve dignity in every situation.

• Just Call Me Fred •

30

I've always liked this Carl Sandburg saying: "Honey, sugar or dung — whatever you're into, some will stick to your fingers."

31

I learned everything from others, especially my father and mother. My dad enjoyed the game of life, yet he undertook debt and obligation seriously.

• Just Call Me Fred •

Hendrik and Fred

32

My dad and I have had more fun than two people are entitled to.

- Just Call Me Fred -

*As iron sharpens iron,
so one man sharpens another.*

— King Solomon, Book of Proverbs

33

People don't want to be managed, they want to be coached. That's why good, intelligent managers are so important.

34

Don't take people by what they say — watch what they do.

35

I sincerely believe that treating others with dignity and sharing our goals and problems has helped a group of common people go far beyond our wildest dreams.

• Just Call Me Fred •

Beijing, 1988

36

Enjoy the culture of others.

37

If the family works well together, understands each other and has a sense of continuity, then you have people you can talk to on a more confidential basis than you can with anyone else. If the family cannot work well together, then the family is a liability.

38

One of the most wonderful things in life is being needed.

• Just Call Me Fred •

Fred and friends

39

Life has been so much fun. I wish I was 25 again and could live another 50 years. I think the best is yet to come.

40

It's not a weakness to say you're sorry.

41

From time to time, we all do stupid things in the heat of the moment.

- Just Call Me Fred -

Gezina and son

42

My parents respected each other. Mutual respect is terribly important in any relationship.

43

You can always tell when you're developing a good team because the members say "we" instead of "I" or "they."

44

It's okay to delegate and it's okay not to delegate — it's pretending to delegate that's disastrous.

- Just Call Me Fred -

45

People will respond to you in proportion to the enthusiasm with which you proclaim your message.

• Just Call Me Fred •

Do not forsake your friend, and the friend of your father.

— King Solomon, Book of Proverbs

46

My dad always wanted to know what type of merchandise we had for poor people. "What are we doing for the people who can't afford all that fancy food." That's one thought that has always stuck in my mind.

• Just Call Me Fred •

47

Team members want to be involved, needed and recognized.

48

My dad liked this old Dutch saying: "It's easy to make good leather out of someone else's hide."

49

A wise man learns from his mistakes. However, it's faster and less costly to learn from someone else's mistakes.

50

If you don't make plans for your successor, you're not doing your job.

51

The bitter taste of poor quality remains long after the taste of a sweet price.

He who pursues righteousness and love finds life, prosperity and honor.

— King Solomon, Book of Proverbs

52

Keep your word at all costs.

• Just Call Me Fred •

Meijer Outlook Show, 1997

Just Call Me Fred

53
Have fun. Leadership isn't always serious.

54

Don't be jealous of people who can do a better job than you can.

55
Asking for help is not a weakness.

56

We are all products of our backgrounds.

57

You're really not an adult until you can accept your parents as human beings with all their mistakes and still love them.

• Just Call Me Fred •

58

I want to leave the world in a little better shape than when I entered it.

59

When you sign a 25-year mortgage, you have to look at the long run, not the short run — and I've signed hundreds in my lifetime so far.

60

When a business closes its doors, it didn't happen overnight. The customers actually fired them long ago.

· Just Call Me Fred ·

61

Where there is harmony, there is strength. This applies to family, business and country.

62
We all have the Peter Principle in us.

63

The more you know, the more you absolutely know you don't know.

64

Is the problem as great as the anxiety or anger it causes you?

• Just Call Me Fred •

• Just Call Me Fred •

As a man thinketh in his heart, so is he.

— King Solomon, Book of Proverbs

65

This is a good business we're in, and I'm enjoying it. I've tried to sprinkle in joy along with the problems. I don't know if I've been successful — I don't think anyone is successful until you look back when you're done and reflect on your accomplishments, or lack thereof.

66

I, like most of us, have a convenient memory sometimes.

67

A person is poor when they have lost the confidence of those closest to them.

• Just Call Me Fred •

68

People respond best when treated as individuals — especially when treated with respect.

69

Addressing each other by name is important. Each of us likes to be recognized as an individual.

70

Our business is like a three-legged milk stool. One leg is the customer, the second is our suppliers and the third is our team members. If you take away one leg, you fall over.

• Just Call Me Fred •

Lena and Fred

71

It seems like I've lived two lives since I was born in 1919. We've gone from the horse and buggy to the Model T, jet planes and rockets to the moon.

72

Don't kill the messenger.

73

The toughest problems can be handled with dignity.

• Just Call Me Fred •

Leonardo's Horse, 1998

74

If you enjoy the challenge of the day, you can have a lot of fun.

75
Delegate, don't abrogate.

76

People closest to the questions almost always have the best answers.

• Just Call Me Fred •

Meijer's Thrift Self-Service Supermarket, 1943

77

In the old days, your word and handshake were all that were necessary in cementing the deal.

78

Companies fail when they lose their desire and ability to compete.

79

Whether we live or die as a company depends on how we meet the challenges of change. Whether or not we meet these challenges depends on if we enjoy them.

• Just Call Me Fred •

Father and son

80

I credit my parents, who gave me my feeling of self-worth.

81

Companies serve many functions. However, no company exists long without profits.

82

We really have two jobs as management: to bring out the best in people in order to help them succeed and to satisfy all our customers so they will want to come back and trade with us.

• Just Call Me Fred •

Meijer Service Recognition Dinner, 1994

83

Everyone wants to feel important.

84

Set your standards — then live by them.

85

It's important to ask questions that cannot be answered with a "Yes" or "No."

- Just Call Me Fred -

Fred with actor James Whitmore

86

*You can't always win.
If you always must win,
you'll end up losing.*

87

*Live up to your promises.
If you can't deliver,
don't promise.*

88

Learn to enjoy and respect each other's differences.

• Just Call Me Fred •

*However many years
a man must live,
let him enjoy them all.*

— King Solomon, Book of Proverbs

89

Live life to the fullest and always be a student.

• Just Call Me Fred •

Fred and Hendrik, 1923

90

Becoming a father is nothing; being one, that's something.

91

We can't reach a goal that we don't have.

92

Everything now being done is going to be done differently, and it's going to be done better. And if we don't do it, our competitors will.

• Just Call Me Fred •

Frederik Meijer Gardens

Just Call Me Fred

93

Take time to count your blessings.

94

I believe I could run almost any company if I was wise enough to listen to the people in that company.

95

People like to know their ideas are taken seriously. Try to use their ideas whenever you can, even if it's one you may have tried before.

96

When you're wrong, admit it.

97

Only ignorant people think they know everything.

98

A steak always tastes better when you get it from your friendly butcher.

99

Whenever possible, promote from within. The person from outside will have their own philosophies. They may have a good track record, but what if their beliefs are counter to how we evolved?

100

We have succeeded by pulling together, sharing our dreams and our worries, having respect for each other and by enjoying life.

• Just Call Me Fred •

• Just Call Me Fred •

101

An industrial psychologist once told me I didn't have the qualities to head a company. Well, maybe not, but we now have more than 115 stores with 75,000 people on our team. Maybe I was just lucky.